POETIC UNIVERSALISMS

Volume I

LENA SMITH CARTER

POETIC UNIVERSALISMS

VOLUME I

Copyright © 2006 by Lena Smith Carter as a compilation of original poetry.

The poems in this work are an original collection of poetry submitted to the manufacturer by the named individual author/publisher. The author/publisher confirms the authenticity of the poetry and the manufacturer is neither liable nor obligated to authenticate.

The views expressed in this book do not reflect the views of the manufacturer or members of the manufacturing staff. These views are solely inured to the author/publisher.

Under the copyright laws of the United States of America, this book is protected, with all the rights and privileges appertaining thereto. This book may not be reproduced, shared, electronically reproduced nor copied by any other means not approved by written consent of the author.

Manufactured in the United States of America

by

www.lulu.com

ISBN: 978-0-6151-3653-0

DEDICATION

To my children:

Ehrika Aileen Carter Gladden
Jessica Faye Carter
David George Carter, Jr.
Blayne Anthony Gladden
Jennifer Mary Gallagher Carter

You continue to make me proud of you with all your sharing, caring, loving, giving, and hard work. I am grateful to God for your successes and know that the future holds only good for all of you. As you know, I do not believe there is anything we do that is more important than working hard to turn out productive citizens for our society. I believe that was done and I am eternally grateful to have been chosen by you.

FOREWORD

In our nation, there are many injustices which occur everyday. We seem to be overrun by violence, murder, war, broken relationships, failures, deceptive politicians, failing schools, et.al. However, one thing is certain: We still have peace here on the homefront, although we have had a few blemishes. The children still play, they still sing songs, and aren't we lucky as a nation to be able to sit with them in the park; have the opportunity to consider such brilliant pastimes as concerts, ballets, opera, sporting events, vacations, art shows, movies, creative writing, and poetry.

We can fully participate or simply participate as a spectator, for "when the tree falls in the forest, if you didn't hear it, did it still fall?" If your son or daughter writes a beautiful, passage, will that talent be magnified or stifled? You have the power to encourage or crush their ambition. Do not always take what you see at face value. Remember the greatest poets of all time often had hidden meanings that could only resonate when experience allowed your understanding of the words and deeply felt emotions.

When we start to complain, we should remember that many people die every day for the freedoms that we enjoy and that every day spent making life better for others especially through creative writing, music, dance, poetry, shows, operas, ballets, etc., is a treasure that we are afforded; we should nurture those tendencies in our children.

This book of poetry explores life's journey in single-word titles and if you have lived any of life, you will see yourself in these pages. Subsequent volumes will explore two-word titles, three-word titles, etc. There will be ten-twenty volumes and hopefully they will remind you of some of your life's happiest times!

                                    Lena Smith Carter
                              dseyafanel@hotmail.com

BEAUTY

(For Patience)

Gilded marble, prismatic glass, hard stone and cool

Has limited beauty minus the sculptor's tool

For beauty, as told by all,

Can have no meaning for some,

But in the fall, winter, and all,

The souls of those who search for

An intangible yet identifiable quality,

May reach for stars and beauty find,

Cloaked in chiseled features, scattered teeth, and

Angular bodies with clandestine secrets yet untold!

KALEIDOSCOPE

Running crystals, red touches,   purple creepers,

yellow stalkers,

green dancers,   myriad rainbow formations!

Delight runs amok

in preview

of this ever changing scenario,   stopped by stops,

returned by turns to challenge

vision's adaptability   to unharness mind's

free-lancing forces at

speeds unimaginable!

ISOLATION

Gone are happy times,

Only thoughts can bring them back,

Sitting here beside the windows

With my cherries in a sack!

I remember all the books we read

That caused our minds to swell

And the poems that we read,

Revealing stories we could tell!

Clocks are ticking and I hear them,

Causing stares I cannot measure,

Will the morning bring some contact or

Even something else to treasure!

Tranquil silence and serenity,

Remain near and close at hand,

Peaceful calm and placidity surround

These spaces and the land.

BENEVOLENCE

Time offers a reprise,

Upon gathering things together,

Quaint offerings to collect

That may please and protect.

Shall I give this?

Yes! You must,

To relieve the grief withheld,

Apportion all the gifts you bring

So that other's treasures swell!

TEMPERANCE

In the middle of the road

is a safer place to be,

Though the edges or the fringes

may be simpler to see.

Can I do this? Often asked

But not facile to reply.

Can I do that? Who knows!

You can choose by and by!

If my choices land me central,

Smoothly I can travel on,

But on fringe and edge supplanted,

There are troubles in that zone!

IMAGINATION

Parallels of thoughts long forgotten,

Seep into my faculties,

Fade from formations

Designed by need

To complete a wanted magnification.

Water, wind, clouds, and dust,

Trace a landscape that must by virtue of its

existence,

Sometimes corral nature's persistence.

Possible? O, through interception,

By space and surface

Portals are lent to intensive speculation.

EQUILIBRIUM

Straight and poised should be your stature,

Level is your head,

Can there be an inquisition launched

Regarding matters dread!

On one side the scales don't balance,

Let my recollection view,

Many matters quite important,

First the moonlight then the dew!

Side to side we pit our wares,

Against the ever-changing tide,

Set parameters, leave a message,

Intelligences undenied!!

INTIMACY

Profundity of emotion!

How deep the trails of

Your touch on my skin!

Chills abound!

Subliminal remembrances

spark slowed responses,

Yet agitation lurks to remind the soul of

Heights, depths, and commitments

To spiritual connections.

The morning dew collects,

Creating froth within my brain,

Sunshine splits the night from day

and I arise again.

Only then does moon appear and raise a semblance

of the night.

Rain and snow and clouds retain their space;

Drop a tender thought.

Only then does my resolve deepen and

Within my space: I recall, the meaning of it all!

ELUCIDATION

Necessity bars an ear from

contemplating complexity in mental leaps,

Conjoined with logic!

Where such occurrences prevail

and logic fails,

The ears perk as the mind assails the

Lingering erudition for clarity!

Intellectual contumacy elicits explication born

Of knowing and the ever present need to know.

PORTENTOUS

Pyramids,

statues,

obelisks,

'scrapers,

and monuments,

retain,

rise,

point,

and signify,

To the exclusion of all else

Events giving rise to human dignity,

Celebratory worth,

Truth,

Lies,

Traditions,

And desires,

All pointing heavenward

defining man's fragility

And conforming to spiritual ideals,

Long appealing to his mortal limitations.

REMINISCENCES

Summer days, meals-a-plenty,

Mystical playmates gathering gently

their wares to return another day to

share again in magnified dreams of elegant castles,

Caught on unknown cliffs

with vast green expanses celebrating life,

play, intrigue, and fun!

Days fly, nights fly,

Everyday I try

to keep light touches of

Years gone by to amplify,

My present thoughts of why

these scenes are nigh;

Enshrouded in tulle-like coverings

projecting childhood images,

Leaving the mind clear,

focused on the unimaginable

of long winters leading to opulent springs!

HOSTILITY

Fomenting emotions surface,

Angst is incurred,

Lending conflict-minded notions

To solutions offered, rendered, and discarded.

Opposition sweeps in,

Crosses lanes of incoming denials

With scathing attempts at acceptance

But rejection creeps to the edge!

LANGOUR

Take a step! No wretched intentions

Yet deep within a painful conflagration engulfs the

energy

Meant to spur this simple act.

In the course of activities,

Complex by day, quiescent by night

As if by magic's exponential assistance,

A partial recovery. . .

Breathe deeply! Rise slowly!

Break the nocturnal fast with water

as first encountered,

Gently rouse waking elements meant to

Soothe recondite depths and raise anew!

GENERATIONS

Through bolstered thoughts

and mirrored features we view

likenesses to observe,

Eyes of green, hazel, gray, and blue

capped by browns,

staying closed-- feeling cascading hair,

Viewing crafted nasal prominences and

cranial angles of ancestors unknown,

Yet seen in curling lashes and grown occlusive

in current faces, foreheads, and jawlines,

Straining to recreate remembrances of

culture   and   family   and

Date anew faces remembered in views gone by.

SYMPATHY

Loss is intrusive

Deafening in its presence,

Intractable in its longevity,

Intimidatory in its fearfulness.

Boldly it gives rise to emptiness,

Serving no master!

Wishes scattered abroad for encompassing

memories long gone,

Experiences indelibly imprinted!

Kindnesses, love, lifetimes gone;

Dreams, notions, passions unfurled;

Missions, relationships, friendship alone

Reveal viscid qualities to a persona hurled.

SOLEMNITY

Crystal, china, gold and silver,
    Stage the atmosphere so grand,
        Only fair and gentle linens
            Add a touch of ecru and tan.

Flowers, etching, paintings all,
  Leave no doubt of things to come,
    Place the ice and lofty grass,
      In a vessel overrun.

Celebrate the tassels and ivory fountains,
  Paint the statues all in gold,

Raise the tapestry, lift the sheers,

    In a celebration bold!

ADORNMENT

Gently place the veil to cover known features,

Add the glimmers and the colors of

lush and fragrant beaches.

Embellish the natural forms surrounding

For a tiny touch of teasing,

Count the flowers, one by one,

Using leaves that alter breezes!

Onyx, emeralds, and lapis lazuli

can and will provide a means

To delight every look on

the promise of a dream

That can garnish the gentle soul,

As it swells with sights untold.

RESOLUTION

Whose time has come? To mire delights,

Refines to meet the seekers truth,

Handled easily with the might

Of weighty years and covert couth.

Promises I mean to keep

Are mired profoundly within the reach

Of good intentions boldly laid,

Amiss by lengths only to fade.

Finally made

Within the span of time waylaid,

I pledge again

to lay the words without a pain

Before the altar free of gain!

LUMINOSITY

Your thoughts alone

Are given to a knowing kind of rest

Upon the pillars of my mind this day!

Tomorrow I shall reason

that they're only temporary,

Lending prominence of an illuminative day.

Points of sheer lucidity,

Conform to mounds of transluscence,

Defining special shades of pink and yellow

Rising to latent gleaming!

RADIANCE

Glowing subtly in a manner unforeseen,

Enter pinks, yellows, reds, blues, and greens.

Bringing prisms ever changing in their hue,

Swinging, swaying, spreading splendor within view.

Luster so illustrious!

Brightness so bold,

Rainbows so elegant,

Beauty untold!

RESPLENDENCE

Expectations raised, gently lending ways,

To praise appearances seen

And antiquities cleaned to perfection

by substances untold,

Yet from secret sources gleaned.

With habitual neck jerks,

Eyes and ears lurk

To find splendor hidden from view

yet tenderly spread in

Defining ways to titillate the resonance

And intensify the vibrations of beauty.

Eclat!

JOCULARITY

Waiting to be told of your arrival!

I sit and stare alone

Hoping to find amidst the fray,

Images present to sway,

Calls for real or imagined candor.

Impossible to conclude

To what extent a clue might grant solutions

Sought without delusion.

Derider, deride!

Portrayer, portray!

Decrier, decry!

To deny means to arrive

Humbled, minimized, and disparaged.

Why do I wait for your arrival?

CORUSCATION

Disturbances engender

Obfuscation of perceived sights,

Left to secure separation by observation

Through creviced spurts and munificent streaks!

Violent bursts,

Meticulous glints,

Intense glitter

Tentative gleams and

Sentimental flashes,

Averted by obstructions

Intent upon a block of constantly beamed light!

ALLURE

Fortune, fame, fortitude reign,

But draw not the tame-spirited

From their lofty perch

As distinction never clouds the space

Claimed to trace the paths of attraction!

Calm, drawn subliminally over intervals,

Graced by desire and formed in fascination

Of ponderous depths!

A quality born of ancestral lingerings,

Buried sweetnesses,

Perceived prissiness,

Beauty of a privet and convergence

Of shades, shadows, textures

Becomes an almost civet-scented incantation.

FELICITY

Craggy, stone clad, and smooth topped mountains
    Faceted amethyst, gleaned from the rough,
    Trillionth cut diamonds, immeasurably
Shining with the brilliance of incandescent sun,
Blazing a trail for arbored glens, ice-laden caverns,
    Deep sea excursions, clay-red banks,
Snow-capped mountains against stark blue heavens
    Laden with unseen billions of stars!
Endless streams run unencumbered over stones,
    Rock cliffs, flowered mounds,
Seeping through crevices florinated by nature's whims.

A vast horizon, stretching beyond vision's expanse,

Dipping slowly to tantalize the presence of celestial orbs,

Focusing attention on deep emotions,

Teeming, yet subdued in contemplation of paroxysmal reaches.

ELEGANCE

Taffetas, brocades, silks, and satins.

The swish and shine and handiwork,

All coiled to spring upon unsuspecting senses.

Creamy colors abound,

wrapping their charms effluently,

Textures are prevalent provoking sensibilities

to exsultant heights.

Folds, flaps, piles, tufts,

Show the decadence exemplified

For probing eyes and tactile ramblings,

Often touched but more often spied!

RHAPSODY

Utterances called upon,

To clarify emotions often unidentified,

And denied.

I expound, delighting

in

the

flow

of

words

tantalized

by

delicious

emotions,

Awed by the resonance reverberating wall-to-wall,

Wary of crisp consonantal conspicuity

Precisely placed and aptly rolled off tongues

To titivate the attendant following!

PASSION

Fleeting rainstorms arouse a scent of natural redolence.

Lightning reminds us of its power,

Thunder cracks our ears in remembrance of scary childhood sounds

And emotions run as deep as the crack of a tsunami.

We are carried along, swiftly raised,

As if by tidal wave and lowered...

Then taken again, as if by whirlwind,

To higher heights! Only to be returned

By the swirls of an eddy!

Tornadoes, typhoons, hurricanes, all,

Thrash water upon the shores

To remind me of your passage

Through these encompassing limbs!

HARMONY

Stand alone and quell the tide of emptiness,

Spread so easily through the masses.

Challenge all oncoming foes yet acknowledge

Their strength in numbers!

Together, they rise to heights unknown,

Creating perfect union through a maze of complexities.

Unknown but admired combinations of mathematical results,

Heard, admired, accepted, and distinguished!

Through aural, emotional, and visual means one is

Satisfied, appeased, entertained, and convinced,

That perceived complexities never go unobserved
and

Mingle in exquisite accord.

JOY

Unbridled impacts released

To bring some consciousness to bear,

Upon the space and time revealed

Kept here without a care.

We celebrate the years anew

Some here and others gone,

Attempts are made to conquer life

Yet we are all alone.

At birth, at death, where is our chance

To mingle in and tone,

Our hearts to perceive the ways of

Cornucopia's cone!

CONTEMPLATION

Pondering what our future holds,

Is difficult at best,

We give, we laugh, we love, we cry,

Defending loves quest!

Our portraits are a token

Of minds intuitively bent

On a communion of oneness,

On our lifetimes spent!

Delving into depths of thought,

No mental stone unturned,

Almost as if a prayer is needed,

To isolate concerns!

ENLIGHTENMENT

Watching, waiting as the opportunities rise,

Climb alone and see the shadows as you go,

Ride the wave of inhibition to the fore,

Tread the air as the waters start to flow.

Swiftly over to horizons gently float,

Mind the castles long surrounded by their moat,

Touch the turrets, structures angled in their way,

Reconcile the passage made within the fray.

Visions, trances, paths familiar day and night,

To a spirit seeking levels yet unseen,

Rapturous phases passed throughout the astral climb,

Leveling out to a state of mind sublime. . .

TENDERNESS

A touch, a kiss, both cause remembrances of bliss,

It gathers lace and silk and velvet 'round the soft

contours.

Bundled and enveloped

With a caring, long caress

Touch my neck, my back, my face,

Then scroll down my longest tress!!

All your words will fall

like

rain,

Touching cheeks so deeply flushed,

And the recent worriment

Fades as if it has been crushed.

MAGNANIMITY

Sacrifice is not the ice,

Of real hearts, cold and dread,

One gives and knows that purpose follows

Offerings sent ahead.

Children eat and lame ones walk,

All spurred by intense flames

That burn along the edges

Of the generous and the tame.

If aid supplies a spirit

With incentive, first to rise,

Then all that came and went before

Lies harnessed down to size.

Donate, give, present, bequeath,

It's there for all to see,

We give, we get, we give again,

We're all that we can be!

SAGACIOUS

Things come and go,

To the mind and heart,

Some remain throughout the years,

Some calm and protect,

Some treat and uplift,

And some allay one's fears!

Seething tides of knowledge flow

And chase the minds of men,

Through centuries unheralded yet

Wrought by civilizations.

They fashion and embellish

Simple concepts grown,

To enhance the mind and free the heart;

Give insight without extenuation.

AFFECTION

My smiles are fresh

in contemplation of your coming,

I stand beside your photo,

bereft of your presence,

Memories float and time conveys

no meaning to frustrations

Felt and worn within the soul

remembering sensations.

Thoughts cannot renew the bonds

yet deep in my distress,

Flourishes the ever-present coil of

life, joy, peace, and happiness.

INVIDIOUS

Many tasks yet to perform,

How does she make them happen,

She moves right through with adept hands

As if finger snapping.

The world looks on in wonder

As she decorates her plan,

To correct to reach, to always impress,

To present as only she can!

I correct, I reach, I attempt to impress

Yet no one seems to observe,

Is prestidigitation in

Her repertoire conserved?

What can I do to reach those heights?

I'll devise a plan that's bold,

To destroy, to malign, and attempt to thwart,

Attentions directed toward her goals!

SECLUSION

Hear the rain, observe the clouds,

Soon the gray will lift,

Wipe the leaf, extend your hand,

Through droplets, it's a gift.

Lounge and gaze upon the scene,

So deftly laid below,

And garner petals for your jar,

Prepare for starlight's glow.

Water surrounds this quiet place,

And laps the distant shore,

Trees sway gently in the breeze,

Crystal 'falls do flow!

Night and day will mingle amiably

Broken only by the bird songs,

And my warning "all is ending"

Is the peal of church gongs!

LOYALTY

Tell the people they are coming,

Do not give details,

Warn them all of their passing,

Leave no sign upon the rails!

Do you know them?

Yes I do. Then you must tell us why

All serious observations

lend no credence to our try,

At gleaning information that is useful to our cause,

"I regret that nothing I know clarifies; it gives me

pause."

Questions, answers, all entwined

as the inquisitions rave,

But if I know, then they won't know,

I will take that to my grave.

TRANQUILITY

Sounds, no sounds, silence

Peace will be found on the quirkiest

ends of phrases, musical reprises

Ease of conversation, thickness of night

Oh, midnight, lend your thoughts to me

And I will find tranquility.

ENCHANTMENT

Butterflies flit!

Red birds sing!

Frogs croak!

The vibrations of hummingbirds ping!

Flowers dance!

Church bells ring!

Snowflakes float!

Celestas sound the ring of kings!

Nature choreographs sights unseen,

That will send the heart a-soaring,

Leaves and blades of grass give pleasure;

Inspiration just by growing!

Yes! Your heart can show its mettle

As bewitching ruses come,

Raise your eyes, calm your soul,

Watch your spirit start to hum!

CAMOUFLAGE

Greens and reds and yellows too,

Claim a place within the view
Of probing eyes that seek to find,
Satisfaction for their mind.

Browns and grays and muted greens,

Lend a helpful hand,
And tans and pinks and pearly hues,
No picnic in the sand!

White can surely cover the forest,

Chase the vision into dimness,
Bleary characters still a-moving
Yet the scene creates distress!

If you cannot turn and find

The entity changing in mid-stream,
All the changes that are made
Will cloak the ever-pending ream!

REVELATION

If I falter while I travel

On life's lonely bitter road,

I'll remember only good things,

That transpired in my abode.

Speak of park scenes and of plateaus,

Mesas, mountains, brooks and range,

All these positive effects

Lend a transient chance at change.

More prescribed things here to nurture

This long journey through the world,

Turn your thoughts to champagne diamonds,

Beaches, oceans, nuts, and pearls!

By what I think I transform life,

I have my way, if I must live,

Nourishing thoughts and claiming space,

I've arrived with much to give!

ANONYMITY

If you hide behind a name,

Or a gilded picture frame,

All who see can then discern

That you only play a game.

If you run through a society,

Oft revered and oftener tame,

You will find the road you travel

Leads to fame; more often blame.

Know the perils of the precipice,

Hide behind the bright sun's gleam,

Your soul rightly breathes in wonder

As new venues flow like streams!

MAJESTY

The organ strikes a chord,

Here's a fanfare loud and true,

The gathering crowd exults,

What are commoners to do!

Gather shoulder next to shoulder

On the crowded avenue,

Watch the carriages approach

On the psyche they encroach!

Mountains transcend vision's reach,

Cottages hold a special place

In the minds of all observers,

Uniquely occupying space.

Rock cliffs dangle, sunsets glimmer,

Oceans rush upon the docks,

Volcanoes simmer, pouring lava,

Heatedly molten mounds of rock!

COMPLAISANCE

Bring the cherries,

Bake a pie!

Bring the food,

Dishes to dry!

Bring the clothes,

Prepare the line!

Bake the bread,

Cracklin's to try!

Bring the books,

Reading to do!

Bring the meat,

Put on the stew!

Bring the newspaper,

Events to follow!

Turn to the "obits,"

Feign sorrow!

Bring the iron,

Clothes to press!

Bring the children,

Time to get dressed!

Bring the knife. . .!!

INTELLIGENCE

Not unseasonable in its arrival,

Not untimely in this place,

Not unfortunate in appearance,

Not unguarded in the race.

Socrates and Shakespeare brought a language

Only experience can understand,

Flowing phrases, stories bounding

As if guided by a hand.

Bach and Handel raised a note,

To communicate and then,

It took Beethoven to complete the cycle

Almost on a whim!

Genius lacks the sensibility

To engage the common thought,

But connects us all so deeply,

Does not really lack for nought.

PARODY

Shadow, me!

Shadow, you!

Count the interval between,

Faces sad and faces happy,

Surely both have had a dream.

If I counter every measure,

Tell this story, if you must,

I will write a composition,

Leave a message in your trust.

Silhouettes expand before us,

See the shape and size appear,

Caricatures leave a heady notion,

Seen in fact, yet drenched in fear!

INDEPENDENCE

Do you need to place an idea
On the channels of her mind,
Draw designs that will remind her
Of the many ways to find,
Tough solutions she'll encounter
Performing many tasks in kind,
"Write the list up", find the courage
To avoid persistent binds!

Separation will be noticed,
But the cycle turns again,
We'll remember where to find
The needed things to ease the pain,
Kneel right down as a reminder
Of positions minus gain,

Rise and contemplate your future;

Your competence never wanes.

INFATUATION

It is April in the hearts of all
Who live upon this stretch,
Yet the inner words I hear
Firmly recollect and etch,
Memories lost and memories stuck
In the annals of my soul,
Only you can reach the depth of it,
April grows cold.

May attempts a weak appearance,
March's winds are hanging round,
But the warmth of earth is calming,
Only rain creates a sound!

Thoughts and ideas are so fleeting,
Did your thoughts come as swift as mine,

You don't come, yet I'll remember,

I will solitarily pine!

BLOSSOMS

Sweet, still, tumescent, small,
We view the fragile blooms
The pinks and reds, the whites enthrall
Passersby at morn and noon!

Evening falls and stars will shine,
The day will swiftly come,
Winds blow the tender petals,
Apples, cherries, roses, plums!

Delight abounds, a zephyr stirs,
Our senses then reveal,
The year, the season, time has come,
No pleasures to conceal.

SOPHISTICATION

Concern for the edges of a crystal vase,

The pearls around a frame,

Sounds received in this my space

Of elemental jazz.

Can elegant enshrouding

Calm the jittery soul,

Wrapping, encircling, swaddling chiffon,

Brings luxuries untold!

Attitude aloof!

Silent stars reveal,

The ever-changing swings and mood

And atmosphere surreal.

Glide within the prescribed arcs,

Sit with majesty!

Rise again! O aloof one

Devoid of tragedy!

DISGRACE

When a story begins

It's often questionable

As to the events and circumstances

Related in the fable.

Mulling over all the thoughts

That brought my mind to shame,

I whisper, sit, and cry alone

Because of all the pain!

There was no truth in some of it

And yet an element rang

With all the peals of unheard bells,

Of chains! Hear the clang?

UNIVERSALITY

Spanning time and seeming often
Immortal in its teeming,
Enveloping elements abound like the
Sunshine in its beaming!

Art, love, music, prayer,
Greed, color, hate and religion,
All needed as an implement
As if an elaborate contagion!

On the canvas, on your chaise,
In your ears and in your pose,
In your heart and on your skin,
In your mind and in your soul!

Be they visual or elusive,

Or emotional in their presence;

They appear and carry substance

Making entrance to our conscience.

COMPLIANCE

Kneeling down beside the road

I see a pilfered treasure,

Lying just beyond me,

And I stop and think and measure,

What this means, should I take it,

Should I just pass by?

From my mother's sagacious arsenal

Of many saws of do's and don'ts,

I take aim at handling gently

Prizes that will not come back to haunt!

Think well!

Remember all!

Protect integrity!

Act reasonably!

PEACE

Doves and olive branches,

Signs of every kind,

Appear so man can n'er forget

"It is the tie that binds."

Children play and sing their songs,

While we wait in the park,

The blessedness of that event

Will really make its mark.

To concerts we will go,

To ballets we'll appear,

All games to view; the skies are clear,

Security is near.

The streams run clear, the clouds appear,

We whisper in the wind,

No nuclear blight, no shadowy sights,

Mutual concord's 'round the bend.

CURIOSITY

We must take the time to stop

And think of questions of the past,

And all new facts that come

Will bring knowledge that will last.

Crystal balls and spider webs

Can sublimate my mind,

And all other prime encounters

Will catalyze in kind!

Billowy clouds, ill-shaped trees,

Thunder and lightning all!

Glaciers in their majesty,

Can icebergs bring the fall?

Awestruck by the myriad mysteries

Which are presently unsolved,

Does the deep desire to know

Cause ingenuities to evolve?

RESTLESSNESS

Time waits for no one,

You chase it day and night,

In dreams you sit and dance and play,

At times you run in fright!

Tension, pressure, passion, pleasure,

All disturb your calm,

Yet reaches for a higher realm

Ignites a new alarm.

Go swiftly now and charge ahead,

Complete the things you must,

Wondering how to stem the tide

From now until you're dust.

EFFERVESCENCE

Lovely biddings stretch before us,

Have a celebration meant

to give a wreath of laurel foliage,

Wrap the scene in dainty scents.

Cheerful dreams are never broken,

Ride the cloud and raze your fears,

All the visions brought before you,

Charm the heart, through all the years!

Energy leads to pure delight,

Carefree choices made to fit,

All the notions, wonders, fortunes

Brought about here, bit by bit!

Bubble over!!!!

DARKNESS

From the abysmal depths to step

And make a mark upon this land,

On the way there is a stumble,

Lift your chin and raise your hand!

Be patient! Check the spectrum,

Out of darkness into light,

Yet the rise from such a piteous spot,

Makes difficult your plight!

Numb and desperate one can cling to

Known and unmistakable pain,

Set the mental construct clear,

Take a "skip in the rain!"

DISOBEDIENCE

Tiptoe past the screen door,

Crawl upon the floor,

It's just a few more inches,

I'll grab it while he snores.

"Who's that out there? Who?"

Comes the interrogation,

I freeze, I sit, I crawl, I slide,

Before the sudden abruption.

Should I return to claim my prize?

I've just begun to ponder,

Peppermint balls and cherry jawbreakers,

All inspire wonder!!

Tiptoe in, make no sound,

Make an extravagant wish,

"Who is that who slithered in and

Clinked the candy dish?"

REBELLION

Listen to the axioms,

Listen to the saws,

Tell me can you follow this or

Does it give you pause!

Review, consider, revise, express,

Dissention without wrath,

Reduce concern for persistent directives

Committed to your path.

Pertinacious in your actions,

Perturbing in your manner,

Vanquish reciprocal collaborations,

Raise high a dissident banner!

PATIENCE

Sitting very quietly

Rocking the wicker chair,

Awaiting your arrival,

Leisurely in my lair.

Branches dipping low,

They tend peacefully to sway,

Cloudy lines across the sky

Melting cares away!

Starlight brightly glittering,

Raindrops falling, splattering!

I'm not anxious in my waiting,

Distant memories calming,

ENDURANCE

Endless years stretch out before you,

Have you weathered adversity well,

Did you listen, did you work hard,

Are there stories now to tell?

Were your talents educible,

Could you contribute without yielding,

Did they elicit awe and wonder,

Leave your soul intact, yet peeling!

Sturdily you climbed and scattered

News of your elusive trail,

Grappling, striving, seeking, finding,

Confirming gains to never fail!

NEGLECT

Left alone to contemplate,

Bygone days and stellar times,

Picturesque scenes come across my mind

As mellow words appear and rhyme.

Gently taking into question

With the new day what I'll see,

Take a long walk, look and listen,

Kick the rocks and rub a tree!

Leaving this secluded station,

I recoil and then show fear

Toward the thought of non remembrance,

Towards the things I've held so dear.

EXCELLENCE

Sit still and things will pass you by,

As others often do,

Renege on active happenings,

And lose a lot or few.

Renew, review, restore your claims

On omnipresent pursuits,

Don't sit, don't stare, don't rest, don't nap,

Wrest boldness from disputes.

Courage rising! Upward! Onward!

Save yourself from apathy,

Stalwart in your pushing forward,

Goals are not in jeopardy.

REINFORCEMENT

Strong stood the pillars of the Temple of Solomon,

Magnificent in its appearance,

The cedars were black, the marble glazed,

The Hanging Gardens danced.

Perchance constituents stood in awe

Of wonders unforeseen,

If so the revelations wrought

Were elaborately keen.

Centuries later buildings stood

With huge constructural "swings,"

Pillars hold, roof tiles bold,

Substantiating things!

PROVOCATION

Stroll along the avenue,

Moist with morning's dew,

Wear your finest garb

Contacts here are few.

From a distant window,

Lips as red as flame,

She watches and she waits alone,

Perched and tame!

She'll bide her time while watching

Your every maneuvering tension,

Mordacious in her style, yet

Intenerate in her invention!

INGENUITY

Work around the hard part,

Bring projects to fruition,

Lay the plan, guard the lines,

Eliminate the condition!

Bright ideas, well-laid prospects,

Clamor for perspective,

Minds expand, imaginations ponder

Solutions and directives.

How to? Can we? All are asked ,

Proposed solutions countered!

This way! Yes! All things considered,

Nothing later floundered!

VIOLENCE

Swiftly you will turn and

Watch the people pass,

Whistles, bells, and sirens all

Require you to think fast!

Your soul is scorched,

Your spirit tinged with each

death knell you hear,

Your blood runs cold as yet another

loses for the year!

The children play for their hearts will not

bear the sadness well,

You hope the senselessness will stop

And killings will be quelled!

Our future will depend upon the measures that we take,

Our history will be written and for our family's sake

We need to spread the message of our extreme malcontent,

and then

"Right the table" of common causes,

give hope to our kin.

NOMAD

Through the craggy rock I climb

Untouched by humankind,

The wolf, the snake, the lizards all

Can search this place and find,

My tracks and scent and long lost hairs

Clinging to makeshift stairs.

The valley lies before me,

The mountains in the great beyond,

Colors beat around trees,

To remind my soul, what's done.

Mother, father, brother, who?

They all are just above

The realm of all that I hold dear,

Mountains, moon and doves!!

PREJUDICE

Mindless anomalies!

Bantering comments!

Hurtful dispositions!

Obstructed vision!

Through the ages men have brought

Their teachings to the fore,

They ruminate and contaminate

Posterity all the more.

Angry visages and angrier words,

Poison to the souls,

That lurch and quiver, tremble, teeter,

Stretched to opposite poles!

The natural state exemplifies good,

The opposite engenders hate,

And in the scheme of exposure,

Perchance: Hades gate?

Born without a worry,

Born without a care,

The legacy they will incur

Conspicuous in their forebears!

SARCASM

Did you measure what was nigh or

Did you even think,

To inquire if all within was well or

Teetering on the brink?

The greenery flourished gloriously,

Yet all you seemed to see,

Were yellow leaves, disfigured limbs,

And knots on cherry trees.

She said, "Today is beautiful!"

And I agree it's true,

Yet pouring forth from scathing lips

Were words to dry the dew!

With all that had transpired, I said

"I love you very much."

And your response was expressionless,

Presented without a touch!

RECIPROSITY

Give me all your love,

Give me all your treasures,

Grant me access to your friends,

What shall I offer, pleasure?

If you refuse, I don't know

What to offer, yet again,

If you accept you give me cause

To turn my face from pain!

It would be good to match your thoughts

And lend my token kiss,

To all that is refined and pointing

To our pending bliss!

TRUST

Will the water that you bring,

Be free and clear of hate,

The foods you gather in this hour,

Be without debate!

The little hand that reaches out

Communicates a need,

To see and feel and touch your face

Without a word or deed!

When your eyes mirror kindness

When your face offers love,

The factors left for all to see,

Delivered from above!

RESENTMENT

Standing alone, late at night

I watched as breezes swirled,

The tables arranged,

The chairs free-standing,

Cloths draping; softly curled.

So many times I've come,

The party is always grand,

The grounds, the streamers,

How gorgeous you look

Is more than I can stand.

Perfection doesn't come often,

In fact it eludes my grasp;

My wish is only for parity,

Which can be secured

As in a pinkie clasp!

ABANDONMENT

Dry was the milieu,

Deep was the basket,

No one knew that right inside,

What could exist? A casket!

Temporarily waylaid

As onlookers passed by,

She rocked and talked and plotted time

To finalize her try.

I still believe it was her fear

That caused this weird decision,

No help, no hope, no tender care

Left her in this position!

My soul and spirit's broken,

But my body still survives,

A chance has come to turn the tide,

New lives to revive!

INTROSPECTION

Gathering my wits:

A half-century just passed by,

I'm drawn to some conclusions,

Can the new one fulfill dreams

And quiet my delusions!

Examine every circumstance,

Continue days on end,

Elaborate upon the findings,

Mental messages send.

Time will flow immeasurably,

And yet I'll need the time

To check, to examine well all thoughts

That came into my mind!

FASCINATION

Mirrored lakes and snowy peaks,

Take our breath away,

Some vast expanses of ocean

Decline into a bay!

Magnolias, dogwoods, cherry trees,

Thrust their scents abroad,

Restructuring our senses,

Some on overload.

Pull petals from peonies,

Tiptoe through the clover,

Delight is found in these pursuits,

How pleasing to the lovers!

RESTORATION

Much is in upheaval,

Night comes super quick,

We run, we roam, and then return

To rebuild brick by brick!

Our emotions bubble over,

Our tangible mem'ries lost,

We look, we sit, we stand, we cry,

As if by nature tossed.

Distant in my memory,

A scene remains transfixed,

It comes and goes and comes again,

Feelings profoundly mixed!

Consistently surrounded by new ideas to make

A replication of something old, yet wanted once

again,

I listen and I labor and never am I idle,

The sweat upon my brow reveals freedom from the

pain.

FANFARE

Trumpets!   Trombones!

Bugles, all!   Play!

The rich sonorities bounce around

Off all the distant walls,

And merriment surrounds the grounds,

Encompassing legions call!

Left! Right! About face,

Commands for all who measure

Formations, steps, and sharp retorts,

All militias treasure.

Up the hills and o'er the plains,

We stand with heads upraised,

The music heard consumes our souls,

The kingdom we will praise!

SUCCESSION

Parades in progress, coaches appear, and
Black-plumed horses dance,
They raise their heads and velvet blankets
Toggle as they prance!

The queen appears, the king is dead,
The servants gather 'round,
Coronation appurtenances all arranged,
How deftly they confound!

The scepter raised, the ring is donned,
Quiet falls like dew,
Amidst the crowds colors blush
In very muted hues.

Born to this occasion,

He stands with glittering crown,

His subjects and the common court

Are gently kneeling down!

DECEPTION

Pregnant with inquiries,

"What did the children say?"

Overrun with niceties,

"How was your day?"

Spawning my perceived importance

At every bend and curve,

Facing situations rising,

Straining every nerve.

For years I spent untold hours

Dressing candlesticks,

Arranging flowers, ironing organza,

Culinary tricks!

What attitudinal aura here

Impressed my weary tasks,

What kinds of things were brought to bear,

Could I now relax?

Our treasures deep within my breast,

Held close, admired by all,

There were no warnings brought to me

That signified the fall!

I wept, I balked, I prayed,

I scoffed, and then I cried,

Preparations singly wrought

Were laid. . . I guess I lied!!

HALLUCINATION

Is a phantasm present,

I thought I was alone,

Yet when I looked, a shadow

seemingly passed, resembling a clone.

A familiar visage floated

Before my very eyes,

The image flitted back and forth

Vainglorious like you and wise.

I'm alone, I know it,

Perspectives can be altered,

Misapprehension deceives me,

Believe me, I faltered.

Illusory patterns make their mark,

Reminiscent of days past,

Transporting minds easily impacted,

Delirium enters fast!

RECOGNITION

Working is a meaningful task,

Done without a care,

Yet one consumed by work alone

Should certainly beware!

We seek our leisure often

And try to find some time,

To inspire deeply, think, relax

Listen to wind chimes!

We return again to complete our tasks

With irrefragable will,

Unequivocal appreciation

Would endow us to our fill!

OBSESSION

Vehemently staring

Across the great divide,

It seems I can't forget

You've been ensconced and still abide.

Deep in my preoccupation,

Runs a gentle stream

Of memories and visions of empurpled horizons,

Oceans geysers teem!

Calm enters and remains

Breezes gently blow,

Orange and golden birds appear,

Reminiscent of halo's glow!

PERSISTENCE

I charge ahead, no second thought

Of what it is that comes,

Lifetimes pass and decades go,

And yet I remain stunned.

Needing some direction

As one often does herein,

I accept some learned discourse,

Ponder deeply the repetitive din.

Goals set,

Goals pursued,

Goals reset,

Goals changed,

Goals lost,

Goals redirected,

Pinnacle reached!!!!

DISSIDENCE

Shocking arguments are made

And friendships really shatter,

Attempts are made at "change of heart,"

But, so far, nothing matters.

Absent from this interval

Agreements will not be advanced,

Opinions gather true momentum,

Never sectile at a glance.

Raging speeches tend to cut into

The mind of innocents,

Causing tension, emotions spent,

Sewing seeds of malcontent!

PERSPICACITY

Trying little words with you,

My intent is clear,

Time is taken to explain,

Eliminating fear!

My patience harnessed.

Care unleashed, to guide you in your climb

To knowledge and cognition

Within a space of time!

Misjudgment of potential

Answers gradually loom,

You take, you rise, and in your mind,

Your grasp remains in tune.

HOSPITALITY

We were welcomed to the inn,

Remaining somewhat wary,

We didn't know this quiet place

And knew we shouldn't hurry!

We walked through glens, along babbling brooks,

And crossed on stones reclined,

We smelled the honeysuckle blossoms

Hanging from the vine.

With that, relaxed and calm,

We then approached the door,

That opened wide and welcomed us,

Tall urns upon the floor.

Tinkling wind chimes pealed,

Tied on sconces room by room,

The fireplace was stacked with logs,

Without impending doom.

DESTINY

Many sets of circumstances

Cross our paths and then,

Lull us on our journey,

'til the bitter end.

No one knows where he goes

Or from whence he came,

Predetermined happenings

Keep him in the game.

Fortune comes to some of us

And others stay dirt poor,

But irresistible powers come

Almost directing a tour!

SATISFACTION

Settled here within these walls,

Vases overrun,

Mahogany, cedar, silk brocades,

Ambrosia freshly done!

Music raises harmonious hope,

The oven brings repast,

Nuts and whipped cream mixed together

Satisfies at last!

Day is done, the night has come,

Don the floor length gown,

Mired in the flannel sheets,

Comforted by the down!

It's day, I'm here, the night is gone,

Impressions to arouse,

Rays of sunshine tempt the panes,

Peeping from the clouds!

MEMENTO

Islands, palm trees, caves, and fog,

Lend a calm retreat,

As I gather drink and handfans,

Mindful of the heat!

Retracing all our deliberate steps,

Time could not erase,

The day we made the auspicious walk

To this memorable place!

Hidden by the oxblood foliage,

Translucent, and quite low,

Carved upon the tree trunk words,

Left here long ago!

INSOLENCE

Little girls so frilly,
Irresistible in their lace,
Nylon shoestrings, buckles all,
Innocence in the face!

They grow and then they change,
Pigtails turn to curls,
There must be something coming...
Impudence unfurled!

Nothing can you tell them,
Without the flounce of skirt,
The shift of eyebrows, tilt of head,
Even the expressions hurt.

Sheer effrontery is her game
Your calm emotions spent,

You try, you plead, then realize,

No words will make a dent!

REFLECTIONS

Blackberries, dewberries, yellow plums,

Occupied our time,

All our walks on dangerous roads,

Punctuated by limes!

Mirrored lakes and tiny fish,

Needles from the pines,

Sumac berries soured our taste,

Strawberries on the vine!

Arriving home we climbed the trees

And sat on opposite sides,

Cherries, cherries, cherries, Wow!

Playtime coincides!

FREEDOM

Close the gate! We've arranged

For no one to depart,

Locks and chains tear minds apart

Helps us steal the heart!

Time moves on and tensions rise,

Families feel the strife,

Men less power feel the drain

And wonder, "What is life?"

Ideas fill the heads of men,

No power brings them pain,

Taken from them they survive

To play the game again!

RETRIBUTION

He's dead, did you know?

He was my only son,

Who caught him and destroyed his life?

Don't worry, "What's done is done!"

How angry is my mindset,

Kindled against the man,

Who dared to raise his hand and take

As only evildoers can!

I haven't heard a new report

Of who has done this deed,

My anger is aroused

And I must follow every lead!

Perhaps it's not my place

To avenge his untimely demise,

But nothing in my purview

Predicts failure; only tries.

POVERTY

Rigors of hardship rising,

The soul is torn and weary,

Eating away at the mind and heart,

Scarcity makes us teary.

Attempting tasks at hand,

We sharpen our skills,

We think the work that's brought to us

Brings wealth, yet really nil!

Is there any way to rise above

The needs that seethe within,

Spirits are downtrodden,

But laborers sometimes win!

Work is never far away,

Being poor is still a mainstay,

One can work and plan another moment:

I pray!

LAUGHTER

Tinkling across the room,

When new faces appear,

Rousing emotions stir inside,

Convulsive sounds are near.

More new faces appear,

Rousing emotions loom

Crinkles appear at corners of eyes,

Tinkling across the room.

Expressions do not clarify

What pleasures here exist,

Yet back and forth the pendulum swings

Participants do not desist!

Spring into action,

Take a stand,

Be readily conversant!

Then plunge in

To create anew

A steady round of merriment!

POSSESSION

Hide this box and tell your friends

You have a new obsession,

Spread new gossip, renounce confidences,

All without regression.

After they have disappeared

Creep silently away,

Reclaim your box and open it,

Take the time to play!

Rub the smooth, cool borders,

Finger recessed chinks,

Shine the impearled surfaces,

To opalescent pink!

Add a perfumed ball,

The butler's patina rampant,

Retain the treasured keepsake,

Effulgence is apparent!

LENA SMITH CARTER

Lena Smith Carter is an internationally traveled concert artist who has sung the poetry of the world in seven languages across America and around the world. She is a graduate of Central State University (OH) with a B. S. in Music Education, a graduate of Miami University (OH) with an M.Mus. in Performance and Repertory, and has studied for her doctorate at the Paris American Academy, Paris, France and The Pennsylvania State University, University Park, PA. Her international travels have taken her from Paris to New York as well as Porto Alegre, RS; Fortaleza, CE; Recife, PE; Joao Pessoa, PB: Natal, RN; Sergipe, AR; and Brasilia, DF, where she appeared at Casa Thomas Jefferson /The American Embassy. Her experiences in the northeast allowed her to use many Brazilian folk songs as both the land and the language are very close to the hearts of northeasterners. In the south of Brazil, where there are many foreign-born citizens who speak other languages natively, she used more German, Latin, Italian, French, and Spanish, as well as Portuguese and English.

In addition to her concert career and international travels, she is a teacher, published poet and author; parent, publisher, patent holder, and philosopher. She has traveled to more than 15 different countries and has had more than thirty-five years experience in the creative arts and education. Her poetry is bold, original, colorful, and imaginative.

You may contact her directly at:

<u>dseyafanel@hotmail.com</u>

Your positive comments are welcome and she will respond with information about forthcoming publications and workshop availability.

www.ingramcontent.com/pod-product-compliance
Lightning Source LLC
Chambersburg PA
CBHW020804160426
43192CB00006B/441